アメリカ英語の発音教本 四訂版

津田塾大学英語英文学科

AMERICAN ENGLISH PRONUNCIATION: A DRILL BOOK

KENKYUSHA

音声について

本書には本文中の音声番号に対応した音声データ（MP3）が付属しており，研究社ウェブサイト（https://www.kenkyusha.co.jp/）から以下の手順で聴くことができます．まず，研究社ウェブサイトのトップページより「音声各種資料ダウンロード」にアクセスし，一覧の中から「アメリカ英語の発音教本」を選んでください．

【ダウンロードする場合】

(1) 上記から聞いたページで「ダウンロード」のボタンをクリックすると，ユーザー名とパスワードの入力が求められますので，以下のように入力してください．

　　ユーザー名：guest　　パスワード：AEPDBT04

(2) ユーザー名とパスワードが正しく入力されると，ファイルのダウンロードが始まります．PC でダウンロード完了後，解凍してご利用ください．

【ウェブ上で聴く場合】

(1) 上記から聞いたページで「音声を聞く」のボタンをクリックすると，ユーザー名とパスワードの入力が求められますので，以下のように入力してください．

　　ユーザー名：guest　　パスワード：AEPDBT04

(2) 音声用のページが開きますので，聞きたい箇所のボタンを押してください．

※スマートフォンやタブレット端末で直接ダウンロードされる場合は，解凍ツールと十分な容量が必要です．Android 端末でダウンロードした場合は，ご自身で解凍用アプリなどをご用意いただく必要があります．

※なお，ご使用の機器によっては，音声がうまく再生されない場合もあります．あらかじめご了承ください．

は　し　が　き

　『アメリカ英語の発音教本』の辿ってきた道を紐解いてみると，1966 年まで遡ることができる．もともとは 1 課に 1 音が割り当てられ，計 46 課から成る教本で，レッスンごとの音源はレコードに収録されていたようだ．その後，この教本の「姉妹版」という位置づけで，1974 年に『テープによるアメリカ英語の発音教本』が出版された．旧著とは異なり，1 課に 1 音ではなく，対照的な音を組み合わせて各レッスンを構成し，計 25 課から成るテキストへと生まれ変わった．また，レッスンごとの音源の記録媒体もレコードからカセット・テープへと替わった．本来ならば，この 1974 年の版を 1966 年版の改訂版，すなわち第 2 版として捉えるべきところだが，レッスンの構成等，全体的に大幅な変更があったことから，この 1974 年の版を『アメリカ英語の発音教本』の初版として位置づけることになったようだ．1974 年の版における執筆には，中島文雄先生とともに，一又民子，一色マサ子，上田明子，大束百合子，天満美智子の諸先生方があたられた．その後，約 17 年の長きにわたり，『テープによるアメリカ英語の発音教本』は多くの大学で採用され，毎年版を重ねた．

　1991 年の改訂新版（第 2 版）では，〈テープによる〉という部分はタイトルから削除されたものの，音源の記録媒体も，テキスト構成も，基本的には 1974 年版のものをそのまま踏襲する形となっている．主だった変更としては，各課で設定されている会話文がリニューアルされ，英語の運用能力がより重視されるようになった点が挙げられる．実際の改訂作業には，Mary Althaus，乾美千代，上田明子，園城寺康子，田近裕子，付岡京子，吉田眞理子の諸先生方があたられたが，執筆者代表には中島文雄先生のお名前が残されていた．

　改訂新版の出版から 21 年の歳月を経て，2012 年に改訂新版（第 3 版）が出版された．大枠は 1991 年の版に則ってはいるが，音声器官や言語音に関する概説を新たに加えるとともに，文強勢やイントネーションなどのプロソディーに関するレッスンも設けた．音源の記録媒体も，カセット・テープから CD へと替わった．さらに，著者名を従来の個人名から「津田塾大学英文学科」という組織名に変更した．改訂作業は主に都田青子が行い，英文のチェックおよび校正は Mary Althaus 先生があたられた．さらに，稲垣善律，奥野晶子，小松雅彦，広実義人，吉田眞理子の諸先生方のご協力もいただいた．

　今回，9 年ぶりに改訂新版（第 4 版）を出す運びとなった．内容は 2012 年の版を踏襲しているが，主な変更点は以下のとおりである：

・「英語の発音への扉」,「英語の子音」,「英語の母音」の 3 部構成とし，前版では巻末に配置されていたプロソディー関連のレッスンを巻頭の「英語の発音への扉」内に移動した.

・共通言語(lingua franca)として世界で用いられる英語の使用領域の拡大に鑑み，新たに World Englishes のレッスンを追加した.

・学科名称の変更に伴い，著者名を「津田塾大学英文学科」から「津田塾大学英語英文学科」とした.

　今回の改訂新版も多くの方々のお力添えをいただきながら完成した. 稲垣善律先生には，校正のみならず，追記箇所の内容についても多くの有益な示唆をいただいた. また，英文の校正ならびに改訂作業に関する綿密なスケジュール管理では，Jonathan D. Picken 先生に大変お世話になった. さらに，奥野晶子，小野雅子，星野德子，吉田眞理子の諸先生方にも実際に授業をご担当いただいているお立場からアドバイスを頂戴した. 研究社との打ち合わせの際の書記係として，また改訂作業に伴う事務手続き等については，学芸学部事務室(TECC・外国語担当)の天野素子さんにご尽力いただいた.

　本書の Lesson 2 と Lesson 3 ならびに「英語の母音」に登場する図はすべて第 3 版の改訂作業の際，当時本学大学院文学研究科の学生であった齋藤瞳さん(現木村瞳さん)，佐々木彩さん，松本茉莉恵さん(現綾部茉莉恵さん)が作成してくれたものをそのまま使用させていただいた.

　最後に，研究社編集部の星野龍氏には大変お世話になった. 企画，編集ならびに校正にいたるまでの各段階において，適切な助言をいただくとともに，本書全体を隈なく丁寧にチェックしていただいた. ここに感謝の意を表したい.

2021 年　9 月

津田塾大学英語英文学科

都田　青子

CONTENTS

発音記号一覧表

子音 (Consonants)

[p]	pit	[pít]				
[b]	bee	[bíː]				
[t]	tooth	[túːθ]				
[d]	dish	[díʃ]				
[k]	come	[kʌ́m]				
[g]	go	[góʊ]				
[f]	full	[fúl]				
[v]	visit	[vízɪt]				
[θ]	thin	[θín]				
[ð]	this	[ðís]				
[s]	sand	[sǽnd]				
[z]	zoo	[zúː]				
[ʃ]	shoe	[ʃúː]				
[ʒ]	vision	[víʒən]				
[ʧ]	church	[ʧɚ́ːʧ]				
[ʤ]	jaw	[ʤɔ́ː]				
[h]	how	[háʊ]				
[m]	man	[mǽn]				
[n]	note	[nóʊt]				
[ŋ]	thing	[θíŋ]				
[r]	right	[ráɪt]				
[l]	late	[léɪt]				
[j]	yet	[jét]				
[w]	watch	[wáʧ]				
[hw]	what	[hwát]				

母音 (Vowels)

単母音

[iː]	beat	[bíːt]
[ɪ]	bit	[bít]
[ɛ]	bet	[bét]
[æ]	bat	[bǽt]
[ɑː]	calm	[káːm]
[ɑ]	bomb	[bám]
[ɔː]	law	[lɔ́ː]
[uː]	pool	[púːl]
[ʊ]	pull	[púl]
[ʌ]	cup	[kʌ́p]
[ɚː]	bird	[bɚ́ːd]

二重母音

[eɪ]	bake	[béɪk]
[aɪ]	time	[táɪm]
[ɔɪ]	boil	[bɔ́ɪl]
[aʊ]	house	[háʊs]
[oʊ]	low	[lóʊ]
[ɪɚ]	fear	[fíɚ]
[ɛɚ]	fare	[féɚ]
[ɑɚ]	far	[fáɚ]
[ɔɚ]	more	[mɔ́ɚ]
[ʊɚ]	tour	[túɚ]

弱母音

[ə]	welcome	[wélkəm]
[ɚ]	sugar	[ʃúgɚ]
[i]	study	[stʌ́di]
[ɪ]*	pocket	[pákɪt]
[u]	actual	[ǽkʧuəl]
[ʊ]*	fortune	[fɔ́ɚʧʊn]

アクセント記号

[´] 第1アクセント，[`] 第2アクセント　例: educate [éʤʊkèɪt]

*単母音 [ɪ], [ʊ] と同じ記号を用いるが，アクセントを受けない音節に現われることから，実際の発音はより弱く，あいまいな響きを持つ.

vi

英語の発音への扉

Lesson 1

World Englishes

今日，共通言語(lingua franca)として世界各地で用いられている英語は，その使用領域の拡大にともない，それぞれの地域や社会の影響を受けながら，より一層多様性を増している．

このような状況においては，英語母語話者の使用する英語のみが「本物の英語」と考えるのではなく，英語母語話者とは異なる，非母語話者の使用する英語についても，その多様性を尊重していくことが重要である．

バラエティに富んださまざまな「英語」をお互いに理解し合えるように使っていこう，というのが1980年代から出てきた World Englishes（世界諸英語）の基本的な考え方である．

1. 国際語としての英語が確立されるまで

今日，世界の共通言語として使われている英語は，5世紀にアングル族が北ヨーロッパからブリテン島に定住した時にはじまったとされている．English という語自体，「アングル族の」を意味する Englisc に由来する．

17世紀半ばから，英国が北米，インド，南アフリカなどをつぎつぎと植民地化するにつれ，英語を母語とする人の数も増えた．14世紀末には約225万人足らずだった英語の母語話者は，20世紀初めには約1億5千万人にまでなったといわれている（中尾・寺島 1988: 3）．今日では，その数は4億人*に達しているともいわれているが，単に母語話者の数が多いという理由だけでは，英語は世界の共通言語としての地位を築くことはできなかった．世界の経済，政治，商業，文化において中心的な役割を果たすようになり，第二言語として，あるいは外国語として日常的にその言語を用いている人の数が多くなったことで，英語は国際語とみなされるようになった．

---

*財務総合政策研究所のデータによる（2020年11月時点）

https://www.mof.go.jp/pri/publication/research_paper_staff_report/staff15.pdf

World Englishes を同心円モデルとして捉えるならば，図1のようになる：

内円（Inner Circle）

　　英語を母語として使用する社会：英国，米国，オーストラリア，カナダなど

外円（Outer Circle）

　　英語を第二言語（多くの場合公用語）として使用する社会：ガーナ，インド，シンガポール，スリランカなど，多くは英語圏の国の旧植民地

拡大円（Expanding Circle）

　　外国語として英語を学ぶ社会：日本を含む多数の国々

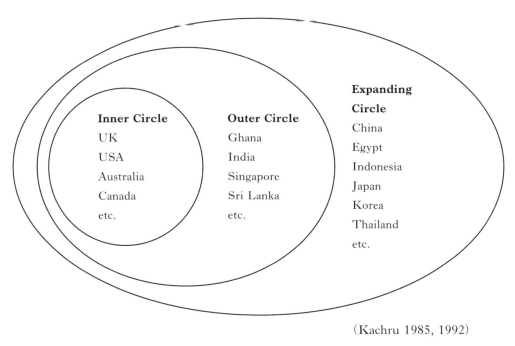

（Kachru 1985, 1992）

図1：英語の同心円モデル

従来の英語教育は，主に内円にのみ焦点を当てていたが，World Englishes の時代における英語を正しく理解するためには，内円だけではなく，外円，さらには拡大円をも考慮した視点をもつことが求められる．

2.　World Englishes の時代における英語学習

英語を学ぶ際，英国や米国など，図1の「内円」に属す英語母語話者とやりとりをすることしか想定していない学習者は意外と少なくない．しかし，英語がコミュニケーションの手段として幅広くさまざまな領域において中心的な役割を果たしている以上，

コミュニケーションの相手は英語の母語話者(内円に属す人)だけではなく，英語を第二言語として使用する人(外円に属す人)や，英語を外国語として学んでいる人(拡大円に属す人)にも及ぶ．つまり，英国や米国といった英語圏の英語だけが「本物の英語」と考えるのは必ずしも妥当とはいえず，それぞれの言語や文化の影響を受けた，英語母語話者とは「異なる英語」も英語母語話者の英語と同等のものとして，その多様性を尊重する姿勢が求められる．つまり，国際語としての英語の役割は以下のように説明することができる：

"English belongs to the world and every nation which uses it does so with different tone, color, and quality. English is an international auxiliary language. It is yours（no matter who you are）as much as it is mine（no matter who I am）. We may use it for different purposes and for different lengths of time on different occasions, but nonetheless it belongs to all of us." (Smith 1983: 2)

ただし，これは実際に英語を使用する場面においての話であり，非母語話者が英語を学習する際には，やはり何らかの「モデル」を拠りどころとすることになる．つまり，World Englishes 時代といえども，しかるべき英語の「モデル」に沿って学習すること自体，否定されるべきではない．

3.　「モデル」となるさまざまな英語

ひとくちに「英語」といってもさまざまな種類のものが存在する．英国，米国，オーストラリア，カナダなど，英語を母語とする国は複数あり，また，それぞれの国ごとに好んで使われる語彙や表現あるいは発音などが大きく異なる場合がある．ここで問題となるのが，これらのいわゆる「内円」に属す国で用いられる英語のどれを学習する際の拠りどころとするか，ということだ．

英語圏の中でも，日本の英語教育の現場では特にアメリカ英語が「モデル」とされることが多い．

もともとアメリカ英語はイギリス英語から派生したものであるが，両者を比べてみると，アメリカ英語の方が，イギリス英語よりも，地域方言間の差異が比較的少ないといわれている．これに対し，イギリス英語には，地域方言に加え，階級制を反映した社会方言も存在している．外国語として英語の発音を学ぶ際には，まずアメリカ英語から始める方が学習しやすいとされているのは，このようにイギリス英語よりも均質化が進んでいるためである．

〈コラム〉　　　　　　　　ひとくちに英語と言うけれど…

　米国，オーストラリア，カナダ，ニュージーランドなどの英語は，もともとすべてイギリス英語を源としているが，固有の社会，文化環境等により，それぞれが独特の発達を遂げることとなる．もちろん意思の疎通の障害になるようなことはほとんどないが，語彙や発音などで異なる点がいくつかある．例えば，「歩道」はイギリス英語では pavement だが，アメリカ英語では sidewalk，オーストラリア英語では footpath という．また，発音面でも，母音の後ろの /r/ 音を発音するか否かの違いが存在する．例えば car を /r/ 音なしで [kɑː] と発音すればイギリス英語，/r/ 音を伴って [kɑr] と発音すればアメリカ英語とみなされる．ただし，日本語においても地域によって方言が存在するのと同様に，英語圏にも方言がもちろん存在する．従って「イギリス英語」や「アメリカ英語」の特徴が英国や米国内のすべての方言にそれぞれ観察される訳ではない．例えば，上述の /r/ 音については，英国の一部の方言では発音することもあり，米国内の一部の方言では逆に /r/ 音を発音しないということもある．

　アメリカ英語は，おおまかに北部，中部，南部の 3 方言地域に区分される（図 2）．この中でも，特に中部方言が代表的な発音とみなされていることから，本書でもこの発音を参考としている．

図 2：アメリカの地域方言

Lesson 2

Speech Organs

1. 音声器官

言語音を作るためには，次の図 3 に示すような音声器官 (speech organs) を用いる.

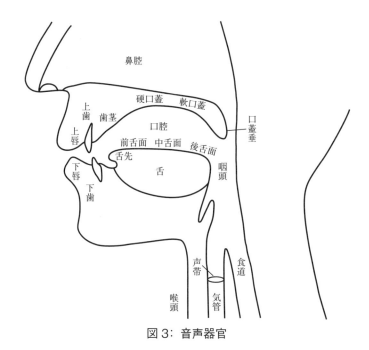

図 3: 音声器官

<ruby>口腔<rt>こうくう</rt></ruby>：いわゆる口の中の空間のことで，共鳴腔としての役割を果たすとともに，調音について果たす役割が大きい．口腔内にある器官は以下のとおりである：
<ruby>舌<rt>ぜっせん</rt></ruby>(舌先(舌尖)，<ruby>前舌<rt>ぜんぜつ</rt></ruby>，<ruby>中舌<rt>ちゅうぜつ</rt></ruby>，<ruby>後舌<rt>こうぜつ</rt></ruby>)；唇(上唇，下唇)；歯(上歯，下歯)；
歯茎；<ruby>口蓋<rt>こうがい</rt></ruby>(<ruby>硬口蓋<rt>こうこうがい</rt></ruby>，<ruby>軟口蓋<rt>なんこうがい</rt></ruby>，<ruby>口蓋垂<rt>こうがいすい</rt></ruby>)

6

鼻腔：鼻の空間のことで，共鳴腔としての役割を果たすとともに，鼻音と呼ばれる音群をつくる上で重要となる．

咽頭：喉頭の上に位置し，共鳴腔の役割を果たす．

喉頭：俗にいう「のど」のことで，その中に声帯をおさめている．

2. 有声音と無声音

言語音は，声帯の振動を伴うかどうかにより，有声音(voiced sound)と無声音(voiceless sound)に分類される．声帯とは，喉頭（のど）に位置している水平な唇状のひだのことをいう．

有声音の場合，声帯は軽く閉じた状態にあるため，左右のひだの間にわずかな隙間ができる（図 4 の固閉じ状態(a)にはない隙間が(c)にあることに注目）．このわずかな隙間を呼気(つまり肺からの空気)が通過することで声帯が振動し，声が生成される．一方，無声音の場合，声帯は大きく開いた状態にあるため（図 4 (b)），呼気が通過する際に声帯は振動せず，声は生成されない．

(a) 固閉じ　　　　　　(b) 無声音　　　　　　(c) 有声音

図 4：声帯の状態

3. Contrast

[p]—[b]	[t]—[d]	[k]—[g]
park—bark	time—dime	cap—gap
pest—best	tip—dip	coat—goat
pill—bill	town—down	kilt—guilt

音声
2

Lesson 3

Speech Sounds

1. 音の分類

喉頭を通過した呼気は，有声と無声の区別があるだけで，まだそれぞれの言語音特有の音質はない．口腔内のどこかで呼気を妨げて作り出される音を子音（consonant）とよび，口腔内のどこにもそのような妨げがなく発せられる音を母音（vowel）という．

2. 英語の子音

子音は3つの基準によって分類される:

1) 口腔内の「どこで」呼気の流れが妨げられるか（調音位置）.
2) 口腔内で「どのように」呼気の流れが妨げられるか（調音法）.
3) 声帯振動の有無.

調音法	調音位置							
	両唇音	唇歯音	歯音	歯茎音	硬口蓋 歯茎音	硬口蓋音	軟口蓋音	声門音
破裂音 （閉鎖音）	p b			t d			k g	
摩擦音		f v	θ ð	s z	ʃ ʒ			h
破擦音					tʃ dʒ			
鼻音	m			n			ŋ	
側音				l				
半母音	w			r		j	(w)*	

図5: 英語の子音分類表

---

*[w] が2つの調音位置に出てくるが，これは唇を丸くして突き出し，同時に後舌部を軟口蓋の位置に上げるからである.

この３つの基準に基づいて英語の子音をまとめると図５のようになる．同じ枠内に２つの子音が入っている場合は，上段が無声音，下段が有声音である．

3. 英語の母音

母音は，呼気が妨げられることなく発せられる音である．口腔内における舌の位置と，舌および唇の状態に基づき，以下の４基準によって分類される：

1) 調音の際に舌がもっとも高くなる位置が前寄りか，後ろ寄りか．
2) 調音の際に舌がもっとも高くなる位置が高いか，低いか．
3) 調音の際に舌が緊張しているか，弛緩しているか．（緊張―弛緩）
4) 調音の際に唇を丸くするか，しないか．（円唇―非円唇）

図６はアメリカ英語と日本語の基本母音をまとめたものである．便宜的に日本語の５母音はカタカナで表記してある．

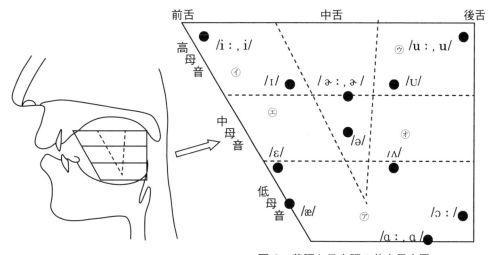

図６：英語と日本語の基本母音図

上記の単音に加え，英語には次の５つの二重母音（diphthongs）がある*：

/eɪ/   *ai*m, br*ea*k, n*eigh*bor, pl*a*y, r*a*dio, v*ei*l

/aɪ/   adv*i*ce, b*uy*, d*y*e, fl*y*, g*ui*de, h*igh*, *is*le

/ɔɪ/   empl*oy*er, n*oi*se

/aʊ/   d*ou*bt, dr*ough*t

/oʊ/   b*oa*t, br*oo*ch, d*ough*nut, gr*ow*, *o*ld, s*ou*l

---

*音声表記は角カッコで囲み（例：[eɪt]），音素表記は斜線で挟むことになっている（例：/eɪt/）が，本書では両表記を区別する必要がない限り，角カッコを用いることとする．

Lesson 4

Word Stress

語の内部には，通常目立つ要素がある．ほかよりも際立つこのような要素を語強勢という．世界の言語は，英語のように強弱による強勢アクセント（stress accent）の言語と，日本語のように高低によるピッチアクセント（pitch accent）の言語に大別される．英語では，強勢を受けた音節に現れる母音を強母音（strong/full vowel）といい，強勢を受けない音節に現れる母音を弱母音（weak/reduced vowel）という．特に弱母音は日本語には存在しないため，英語の弱母音をいかに弱く，短く，曖昧な音色で発音するかがポイントとなる．

1. Words

Pay careful attention to the differences between the strong and weak vowels.

about [əbáʊt]	apostrophe [əpástrəfi]	attend [ətɛ́nd]
because [bɪkɔ́ːz]	business [bíznəs]	charity [ʧǽrəti]
city [síti]	company [kʌ́mp(ə)ni]	data [déɪtə]
engage [ɪngéɪʤ]	everybody [évribàdi]	examine [ɪgzǽmɪn]
express [ɪksprés]	future [fjúːʧɚ]	mother [mʌ́ðɚ]
operetta [ùpərétə]	opinion [əpínjən]	orchard [ɔ́ɚʧɚd]
regular [régjʊlɚ]	torture [tɔ́ɚʧɚ]	visual [víʒuəl]

2. Phrases

above all—Above all, he likes us to be punctual.

hurry up—If you don't hurry up, we'll be late.

office hours—The professor's office hours are from 3:00 to 5:00.

take it easy—Take it easy. We have plenty of time.

3. Strong form vs. Weak form

一般的に，単語は内容語(content word)と機能語(function word)に分類される．内容語は，名詞，動詞，形容詞，副詞，指示代名詞，疑問代名詞，疑問副詞，感嘆詞など内容を担う語のことを指す．一方，機能語は，主に文法的な役割を果たしており，それ自体ほとんど意味をもたない．機能語の中には代名詞，冠詞，前置詞，助動詞などが含まれる．

英語の場合，内容語は孤立した状態においても文中に現れる場合でも，変化することなく，同じように発音される．しかし，機能語は，孤立した時の発音と文中に現れる場合の発音が異なる．孤立した時の発音を強形(strong form)，文中での弱い発音を弱形(weak form)という．

Ann used to talk to the manager a lot.

(a) 強形　　　　　[æn juːst tuː tɔːk tuː ðiː mænɪdʒɚ eɪ lɑt]

(b) 弱形　　　　　[æn juːstə tɔːk tə ðə mænɪdʒɚ ə lɑt]

上の例文で，すべての語を強形を用いて発音した(a)よりも，機能語を弱形で発音した(b)の方が自然な英語のリズムになることがわかるだろう．

強形と弱形の交替現象は助動詞や be 動詞の肯定形と否定形との間にもみられ，肯定形の場合は弱形が用いられるが，否定辞 not とともに否定文では強形が用いられる．

〈肯定文 (weak form)〉	〈否定文 (strong form)〉
Jack and Jill **have** left for Paris. [əv]	Jack and Jill **haven't** left for Paris. [hævnt]
I **can** do it. [k(ə)n]	I **can't** do it. [kænt]
The children **are** ready to go. [ɚ]	The children **aren't** ready to go. [ɑɚnt]
The cat **was** trying to catch the rat. [wəz]	The cat **wasn't** trying to catch the rat. [wɑznt]

4. Extended practice

Bill ⎰ has ⎱ been able to find the book that you were looking for.
⎱ hasn't ⎰

Margaret ⎰ was ⎱ surprised to hear that her son wanted to go to L.A.
⎱ wasn't ⎰

Lesson 5

Sentence Rhythm

リズムは，同じ構造が繰り返されることによって生み出されるものである．音楽の世界にもさまざまな異なるリズムの曲が存在するように，ことばの世界にも，言語ごとに独特のリズムが存在する．

1. Stress-timed rhythm vs. Syllable-timed rhythm

言語のリズムは，ほぼ等しい間隔をおいた音の強弱や高低などが繰り返されることで生み出される．世界の言語は，繰り返される言語構造に応じて，一般的に強勢拍リズム（stress-timed rhythm）の言語と音節拍リズム（syllable-timed rhythm）の言語に大別される．前者は，強勢アクセントを担う音節が相対的にほぼ等しい時間間隔で繰り返し現れる（例：英語，オランダ語，ロシア語など）．一方，後者は，音節がほぼ等しい長さで繰り返し発音されることで生み出される（例：フランス語，日本語など）．

2. Sentence stress

英語の強勢拍リズムを考えるうえで，語強勢（word stress）が関与していることはいうまでもない．しかし，文ないし句の中で連続体として用いられる場合，内容語は語強勢を保持するのに対し，機能語は特殊な場合を除いて，原則として自身が本来もつ語強勢を失い，弱く発音される．つまり，英語では，語強勢と，文中で単語が担う強勢，すなわち文強勢（sentence stress）は分けて考える必要がある．（⇨Lesson 4 参照）

(a) Dogs eat bones.

(b) The dogs eat the bones.

(c) The dogs will eat the bones.

(d) いぬ

(e) いぬとねこ

(f) いぬとねこがすき

(a)，（b），（c）の順にだんだんと語数が増えるが，文強勢を担う内容語（dogs, eat bones）の数は変わらないため，これら3文を発音するのに要する時間はほぼ同じである．これに対し，日本語は各音節（より厳密にはモーラという単位）がほぼ等しい長さで発せられるので，語数が増えれば，音節数も当然増え，発音に要する時間は長くなる．つまり，（d）よりも（e），（e）よりも（f）の発音に要する時間が長くなる．このことから，強勢を担う音節が規則的に現れることで「英語らしい」言語リズムが生まれるのに対し，1つ1つの音節（モーラ）がほぼ等しい長さで繰り返されることで「日本語らしい」言語リズムが生まれるといえる．

3. Sentence rhythm practice

Practice the sentence rhythm of each of the following sentences by focusing on the difference in vowel quality between the content words (i.e.*, the underlined words) and the function words.

1. <u>Cats</u> <u>like</u> <u>rats</u>.
   The <u>cats</u> <u>like</u> <u>rats</u>.
   The <u>cats</u> will <u>like</u> the <u>rats</u>.
   The <u>cats</u> will have <u>liked</u> the <u>rats</u>.
2. The <u>president</u> <u>came</u> to <u>Japan</u> in <u>September</u>.
3. My <u>father</u> had a <u>sandwich</u> for <u>lunch</u>.
4. <u>Jill</u> will be <u>going</u> to the <u>library</u> <u>today</u>.
5. The <u>phone</u> was <u>ringing</u> when I <u>entered</u> the <u>house</u>.

4. Conversation

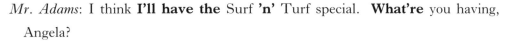

At a restaurant

Mr. Adams: I think **I'll have the** Surf 'n' Turf special. **What're** you having, Angela?

Mrs. Adams: I **can't** really decide . . . the Wild West Burger with French Fries sounds so tempting, but then, **Fish 'n' Chips** is always a good, safe choice, if you know what I mean.

Mr. Adams: Of course, at least with **Fish 'n' Chips** you know what to expect! If I were you though, **I'd go for the** Wild West Burger—be adventurous!

Mrs. Adams: No . . . I guess **I'm not in an** adventurous mood today. I'll have **the Fish 'n' Chips**, after all.

---

*i.e. ラテン語の id est の略.「すなわち，言い換えれば」の意.

Lesson 6

Intonation

疑問文や平叙文を区別し，話者の感情を表すのに用いられる声の調子，つまり音の高低をイントネーション（音調）という.

1. Intonation patterns

イントネーションは，相対的に4つのレベルに分けられる．このうち，4のレベルは驚きなど特に強い感情を表す時以外には用いられず，通常は3以下のレベルを用途に応じて使い分ける．これらのレベルを以下抑揚線で表す.

Linda is going to study in ⌐Canada.

_____ 4（特高，extra high）
_____ 3（高，high）
_____ 2（中，mid）
_____ 1（低，low）

イントネーションの主だった種類をまとめると以下のようなものがある.

 （1）**下降調**（falling intonation）：平叙文，命令文，感嘆文に現れる型.

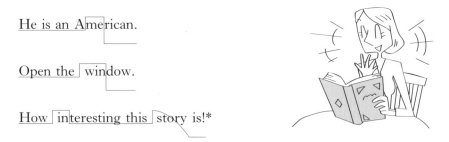

He is an A⌐merican.

Open the ⌐window.

How ⌐interesting this ⌐story is!*

---

*高低の移行は，音節間の切れ目で行われるのが一般的だが，単音節語など音節内部で高低の移行が行われる場合は縦のまっすぐな線ではなく，曲線を用いる.

(2) **上昇調**（rising intonation）：疑問文などに見られる型.

Do you like to study English?

I beg your pardon?

(3) **下降上昇型**（falling-rising intonation）：平叙文（ためらい），依頼の意味を表す命令文に現れる型.

You may be right, I suppose.

Shut the window, will you?

(4) **上昇下降型**（rising-falling intonation）：選択疑問文，3つ以上列挙する平叙文に現れる型.

Do you like carrots or cucumbers?

She's very fluent in English, French, and Italian.

2. Intonation practice

1. My father came home early.
2. Did he come home early?
3. Is this your book?—Yes, it is.
4. Whose book is this?—It's Judy's.
5. Is this yours or mine?—It's yours.
6. You can come with us, or you can stay home.
7. What a large house that is!

3. Conversation

A.

Bill: What shall we have for lunch?

Emi: There are so many restaurants nearby, it's hard to decide, isn't it?

Bill: Quite true. We could choose from French, Italian, Chinese, or Vietnamese food.

Emi: How about Italian?

15

Bill: That sounds good. Let's go!

B.

Martin: Oh no! The government wants to raise taxes again, the newspaper says. I can't stand it any longer!

Catherine: But, Martin, if the money's put to good use, I don't think anyone should object to the government's proposal.

Martin: Don't be ridiculous, Catherine! We're paying enough already!

Catherine: Taxes *are* high, but don't forget they do help in providing a good education for our children.

4. Extended practice

The torch of wisdom and knowledge passes from hand to hand, from generation to generation. We are only bearers of it for a short space of years, but it must pass on to others with its sacred flame ever bright, ever rekindled afresh.

Whether as teachers or home-makers, your duty is equally great. Do not let your light grow dim—carry your torch eagerly and bravely your allotted time and distance, kindling it anew, and then make sure that you pass it on to others who are coming after you.

> (Excerpt from "The Principal's Address to the Graduating Class of 1912," Tsuda University, by Umeko Tsuda)

〈コラム〉　　津田梅子(1864 年 12 月 31 日—1929 年 8 月 16 日)

　女子英學塾(現在の津田塾大学)の創立者。女性の地位向上こそ日本の発展につながると信じ,「男性と協力して対等に力を発揮できる,自立した女性の育成」を目指し,女性の高等教育に生涯を捧げた。

英語の子音

Lesson 7

[p]—[b]

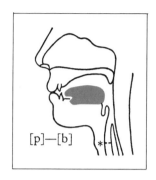

[p] は日本語の「パ行」，[b] は「バ行」の子音とほぼ同じと考えてもよい．ただし，強勢のある音節の最初にあり，なおかつ母音に直結する [p] は気息音（aspiration）を伴うため，強めの呼気で発音する必要がある．逆に，語尾の [p]，[b] は弱く，特に前者は閉鎖されたまま破裂しないで発音されることが多い．

1. Words

[p]

Initial	Medial	Final
pearl [pə́ːl]	napkin [nǽpkɪn]	Europe [jú(ə)rəp]
pigeon [pídʒən]	opposite [ápəzɪt]	scholarship [skálərʃìp]
pot [pát]	temple [témpl]	sleep [slíːp]

[b]

Initial	Medial	Final
balloon [bəlúːn]	album [ǽlbəm]	crab [krǽb]
bless [blés]	autobiography	grab [grǽb]
Buddhism [búdɪzm]	[ɔ̀ːtəbaɪágrəfi]	rib [ríb]
	fiber [fáɪbər]	

2. Phrases

baked potatoes—Let's have steak and baked potatoes for dinner.

blueberry pie—How about some blueberry pie for dessert?

a beautiful princess—Once upon a time, there lived a beautiful princess with long
　　black hair.

18

3. Contrast

[p]—[b]

park—bark	pie—buy	cap—cab
peach—beach	pig—big	mop—mob
pest—best	pill—bill	nip—nib
pet—bet	pull—bull	tap—tab

4. Extended practice

A.   Betty Botter bought some butter,

"But," said she, "the butter's bitter;

If I put it in my batter,

It will make my batter bitter,

But a bit of better butter,

Will make my batter better."

(Mother Goose)

B.   Peter Piper picked a peck of pickled peppers,

A peck of pickled peppers, Peter Piper picked.

If Peter Piper picked a peck of pickled peppers,

How many pickled peppers did Peter Piper pick?

(Mother Goose)

5. Conversation

At the airport

Wife: We have to go through passport control, dear.

Husband: You've got our passports, right?

Wife: No, I don't have them, you do. I saw you put them in your pocket.

Husband: Are you sure? Let me see . . . here's a pen . . . a pencil . . . my pipe, but no passports . . . .

Wife: Probably you left them on the plane. We'd better go back and check.

Husband: Perhaps you're right. I'll go ask.

Lesson 8

[t]—[d]

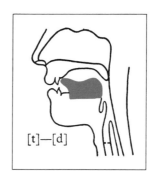

[t]—[d]

厳密に言うと，/t, d/ は日本語と英語とでは調音位置が若干異なるが，英語の [t] は日本語の「タ，テ，ト」，[d] は「ダ，デ，ド」のそれぞれの子音で代用して差し支えない．また，[p] 同様，[t] も強勢のある音節のはじめに来て母音に直結する場合は，気息音を伴って発音され，語尾の位置では破裂されない傾向にある．

1. Words

[t]

Initial	Medial	Final
temperature [témp(ə)rətʃ ùɚ]	letter [létɚ]	fault [fɔ́ːlt]
tropical [trúpɪk(ə)l]	notice [nóʊtɪs]	shout [ʃáʊt]
twilight [twáɪlàɪt]	satisfy [sǽtɪsfàɪ]	sweat [swét]

[d]

Initial	Medial	Final
damage [dǽmɪʤ]	academic [ӕkədémɪk]	crowd [kráʊd]
deliver [dɪlívɚ]	endless [éndləs]	forward [fɔ́ɚwɚd]
dentist [déntɪst]	kidnap [kídnæp]	spread [spréd]

音声 16

2. Phrases

a hot day—According to the weather forecast, tomorrow will be a hot day.

medical treatment—I think he needs medical treatment right away.

time and tide—Time and tide wait for no man.

20

3. Contrast

[t]—[d]

tip—dip	try—dry	tale—dale
touch—Dutch	town—down	time—dime
trunk—drunk	fate—fade	coat—code
neat—need	seat—seed	bet—bed

4. Extended practice

A.　When a doctor doctors a doctor,

　　　does the doctor doing the doctoring

　　　doctor as the doctor being doctored wants to be doctored

　　　or does the doctor doing the doctoring doctor as he wants to doctor?

(Tongue twister)

B.　A tutor who tooted a flute

　　　Tried to tutor two tooters to toot.

　　　Said the two to the tutor,

　　　"Is it harder to toot,

　　　Or to tutor two tooters to toot?"

(Tongue twister)

5. Conversation

Man: Could you tell me where the toy store is?

Clerk: Certainly. It's just two doors down.

Man: It looks terribly dark down there.

Clerk: Oh, I forgot. It's past their closing time.

〈コラム〉　　　**アメリカ英語で riding＝writing?**

　アメリカ英語では，強い母音と弱い母音に挟まれた /t/ は日本語のラ行音に似た音質となる．この有声化された /t/ は歯茎弾音といい，[ɾ] の記号で表す．例えば，city が「スィリー」に聞こえたり，little が「リルー」に聞こえたりするのはこのためだ．

　英語を外国語として学ぶ者としては，無理にこの発音を習得する必要はないが，聞き取りの際には注意をしないと，riding /raɪdɪŋ/ と writing /raɪtɪŋ/ がまったく同じように聞こえてしまうことがある．

Lesson 9

[k]—[g]

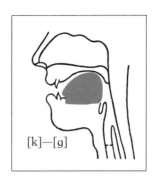

[k]—[g]

[k] は日本語の「カ行」，[g] は「ガ行」の子音とほぼ同じだが，英語の [k], [g] の方が閉鎖も破裂も強い．また，強勢のある音節の最初にあり，なおかつ母音が後続する [k] は気息音を伴って発音されるが，語尾の位置では [k], [g] ともに弱く発音されることが多い．

1. Words

[k]

Initial	Medial	Final
chemistry [kémɪstri]	characteristic	hawk [hɔ́ːk]
comedian [kəmíːdiən]	[kæ̀rəktərístɪk]	skylark [skáɪlɑ̀ː˞k]
keyboard [kíːbɔ̀ː˞d]	local [lóʊk(ə)l]	stomachache [stʌ́məkèɪk]
	rocky [rɑ́ki]	

[g]

Initial	Medial	Final
galaxy [gǽləksi]	agony [ǽgəni]	eggnog [égnɑ̀g]
govern [gʌ́vɚn]	ignorant [ígnərənt]	fog [fɑ́g]
guide [gáɪd]	signature [sígnətʃɚ]	vogue [vóʊg]

2. Phrases

a good command—She has a good command of English.

a college graduate—I am a college graduate.

a guilty conscience—He had a guilty conscience about not having been honest with his brother.

22

3. Contrast

[k]—[g]

cap—gap	cod—god	clue—glue
kilt—guilt	coat—goat	cane—gain
crow—grow	back—bag	cot—got

4. Extended practice

A.   The ghost that got caught in the closet

      Kicked Greta's kettles and cans with great glee

      Till Greta got cross and came to the closet

      And kicked the crass ghost in its knee.

      Now the ghost is gone from her closet

      And Greta keeps close watch o'er the key.

B.   There was a crooked man,

        and he walked a crooked mile.

      He found a crooked sixpence

        against a crooked stile.

      He bought a crooked cat,

        which caught a crooked mouse,

      And they all lived together

        in a little crooked house.

                (Mother Goose)

5. Conversation

Mr. Gray: Congratulations, Cathy! I hear you've been accepted at Cambridge.

Cathy: Thank you very much, Mr. Gray. But actually it's Oxford, not Cambridge.

Mr. Gray: I'm sorry, I must have gotten mixed up. Well, it's great news anyway.

Cathy: Yes, I can't believe my good luck!

Lesson 10

[f]—[v]

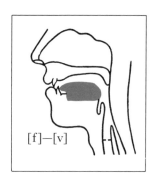

[f]—[v]

どちらも日本語にはない音である．日本語の「フ」や「ブ」の子音は両唇音であるのに対して，英語の [f], [v] は唇歯音であるので，発音の仕方に違いがある．[f], [v] どちらも，上の歯の表面に下唇の内側を軽く触れさせるように発音する．

1. Words

[f]

Initial	Medial	Final
face [féɪs]	safety [séɪfti]	cough [kɔ́ːf]
fever [fíːvɚ]	sofa [sóʊfə]	laugh [lǽf]
forest [fɔ́ːrəst]	trophy [tróʊfi]	wolf [wúlf]

[v]

Initial	Medial	Final
variety [vəráɪəti]	flavor [fléɪvɚ]	dove [dʌ́v]
Venus [víːnəs]	lavender [lǽv(ə)ndɚ]	grieve [gríːv]
volunteer [vʌ̀ləntíɚ]	souvenir [sùːvəníɚ]	positive [pázətɪv]

音声
26

2. Phrases

a fine view—We enjoyed a fine view of the mountains from the window of our
    hotel.

very frightening—There was a very frightening scene in the movie.

fall in love—Romeo fell in love with Juliet at first sight.

24

3. Contrast

[f]—[v]

leaf—leave	safe—save	few—view
fan—van	fail—veil	fast—vast
proof—prove	thief—thieve	strife—strive

[v]—[b]

very—berry	vote—boat	vent—bent
vest—best	verve—verb	vigor—bigger
vanish—banish	vow—bow	

4. Conversation

Philip: Would you like to see a photo of my dog, Fiona?

Fiona: Sure, Philip. What's his name?

Philip: Puffin.

Fiona: Puffin? That's a very funny name for a dog . . . .

Philip: I know, but he looked just like a puffin the first time we saw him.

Fiona: For heaven's sake! Now that you mention it, he does look like a puffin, doesn't he?

5. Recognition drills

Listen to the recording and circle the letter of the sentence you hear.

[b]—[v]

1. a) His speech was about TB.
   b) His speech was about TV.

2. a) He lost the boat.
   b) He lost the vote.

3. a) The queen made a bow.
   b) The queen made a vow.

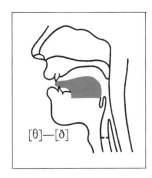

$[\theta]—[\eth]$

どちらも日本語にはない音で，$[\theta]$, $[\eth]$ ともに舌先と門歯の間で呼気を流出させて発音する．日本語の「サ行」や「ザ行」の子音で代用する傾向があるので注意を要する．

1. Words

$[\theta]$

Initial	Medial	Final
think [θíŋk]	mathematics [mæ̀θəmǽtɪks]	faith [féɪθ]
third [θə́ːd]	nothing [nʌ́θɪŋ]	health [hélθ]
thoroughly [θə́ːrəli]	pathetic [pəθétɪk]	tooth [túːθ]

$[\eth]$

Initial	Medial	Final
the [ðíː, ðə, ði]	mother [mʌ́ðə]	bathe [béɪð]
then [ðén]	rhythm [ríðm]	loathe [lóʊð]
those [ðóʊz]	worthiness [wə́ːðinəs]	smooth [smúːð]

2. Phrases

nothing thrilling—Nothing thrilling happened at the party.

Southern accent—His father speaks English with a strong Southern accent.

withered thistles—The withered thistles were still swaying in the cold wind.

3. Contrast

[ð]—[d]

their—dare	breathing—breeding	soothe—sued
then—den	lather—ladder	writhe—ride
thy—die	worthy—wordy	loathe—load

4. Extended practice

I thought a thought, but the thought I thought wasn't the thought I thought I thought. (Tongue twister)

5. Recognition drills

Listen to the recording and circle the letter of the sentence you hear.

A. [t]—[θ]

1. a) It was true.
   b) It was through.

2. a) That's a good team.
   b) That's a good theme.

B. [f]—[θ]

1. a) He will be free soon.
   b) He will be three soon.

2. a) She fought in vain.
   b) She thought in vain.

C. [d]—[ð]

1. a) She didn't like *D*'s.
   b) She didn't like these.

2. a) Can you pronounce the word *den*?
   b) Can you pronounce the word *then*?

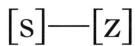

Lesson 12

[s]—[z]

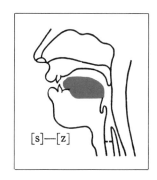

[s]—[z]

[s] は日本語の「サ，ス，セ，ソ」の子音に，[z] は「ザ，ズ，ゼ，ゾ」の子音に近い．ただし，日本語のザ行では語頭の子音に軽い閉鎖を伴うので，zoo [zuː] を [dzuː] のように発音しないように心掛ける必要がある．また，[s] に [ɪ] や [iː] が続く場合，日本語の「シ」につられて [ʃ] を用いないように注意する必要がある．

1.　Words

[s]

Initial	Medial	Final
city [síti]	person [pɚ́ːs(ə)n]	cease [síːs]
smoke [smóʊk]	possible [pásəbl]	mass [mǽs]
stew [st(j)úː]	proceed [prəsíːd]	worse [wɚ́ːs]

[z]

Initial	Medial	Final
zero [zíːroʊ]	closing [klóʊzɪŋ]	franchise [frǽntʃaɪz]
zoo [zúː]	present [préz(ə)nt]	prize [práɪz]
zoology [zoʊáləʤi]	wizard [wízɚd]	shoes [ʃúːz]

音声
32

2.　Phrases

run zigzag—The road runs zigzag through the hills.

amusement parks—There weren't many amusement parks in those days.

a silver spoon—She was born with a silver spoon in her mouth.

3. Contrast

[s]—[θ]

sink—think	seem—theme	pass—path
sank—thank	saw—thaw	worse—worth

[z]—[ð]

Zen—then	closing—clothing	breeze—breathe
z's—these	wizard—withered	bays—bathe

4. Conversation

Sam: Let's go swimming on Saturday!

Sally: I really don't care much for swimming, Sam. I'd rather go to the zoo.

Sam: The zoo? Come on, Sally, that's a place for kids!

Sally: I think it's a great place for both kids and adults. We could go see the snakes and the zebras and . . . .

Sam: Okay, okay, we'll go see the zebras, but not the snakes!

5. Recognition drills

Listen to the recording and circle the letter of the sentence you hear.

A. [s]—[θ]

1. a) She sought it.
   b) She thought it.

2. a) He has a big mouse.
   b) He has a big mouth.

B. [z]—[ð]

1. a) It was Zen that she studied.
   b) It was then that she studied.

2. a) He's talking about closing.
   b) He's talking about clothing.

Lesson 13

[ʃ]—[ʒ]

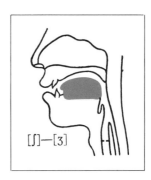

[ʃ] は日本語の「シ」の子音を発音する時よりも，唇をやや丸めて突き出すと，より英語らしく聞こえる．日本語の「ジ」は破擦音 [ʤ] であって [ʒ] ではないので，[ʤ] と [ʒ] を混同して，例えば leisure [líːʒɚ] を [líːʤɚ] と発音しないように注意を要する．

1. Words

[ʃ]

Initial	Medial	Final
she [ʃíː]	negotiation [nɪgòʊʃiéɪʃən]	cash [kæʃ]
shrink [ʃríŋk]	ocean [óʊʃən]	finish [fínɪʃ]
sugar [ʃúgɚ]	precious [préʃəs]	mustache [mʌ́stæʃ]

[ʒ]

Initial	Medial	Final
	casual [kǽʒuəl]	beige [béɪʒ]
	illusion [ɪlúːʒən]	collage [kəláːʒ]
	treasure [tréʒɚ]	rouge [rúːʒ]

音声
35

2. Phrases

shining seashells—She found some shining seashells on the shore.

shine shoes—Mr. Shaw shines his shoes every morning.

an unusual vision—Shirley has an unusual vision of the world's future.

casual association—They enjoyed their casual association with the townspeople.

3. Contrast

[ʃ]—[s]

she—see	leashed—leased	Irish—iris
ship—sip	clashing—classing	lash—lass
shake—sake	meshes—messes	swish—Swiss

[ʒ]—[z]

composure—composer　seizure—Caesar

4. Extended practice

She sells seashells by the seashore.

If she sells seashells by the seashore,

Then the shells she sells must be seashore shells.

(Tongue twister)

5. Conversation

Customer: Does this shop sell Swedish shampoo?

Shop assistant: Swedish shampoo? I'm afraid not.

Customer: It's made with a precious and unusual mixture of ingredients.

Shop assistant: You might want to try the shop on Rouge St.

Customer: I'll do that. Thank you.

Shop assistant: My pleasure.

6. Recognition drills

Listen to the recording and circle the letter of the sentence you hear.

A. [ʃ]—[s]

1. a) He took a ship.
   b) He took a sip.

2. a) I bought a new sheet.
   b) I bought a new seat.

B. [ʒ]—[z]

1. a) The singer lost her composure.
   b) The singer lost her composer.

Lesson 14

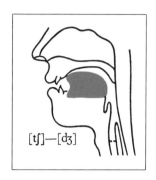

[tʃ]—[dʒ]

[tʃ] は日本語の「チ」に含まれる子音に近いが，日本語よりも呼気が強く，唇を少し突き出すように発音する．[dʒ] は日本語の「ジ」の子音とほぼ同じと考えてよい．破擦音は破裂音（＝閉鎖音）の破裂が緩慢で摩擦になったものであることから，記号も破裂音([t], [d])と摩擦音([ʃ], [ʒ])を組み合わせたものを用いる．

1.　Words

[tʃ]

Initial	Medial	Final
cheese [tʃíːz]	kitchen [kítʃən]	approach [əpróutʃ]
chess [tʃés]	merchandise [mɚ́ːtʃəndàɪz]	catch [kǽtʃ]
chimpanzee [tʃìmpænzíː]	wretched [rétʃɪd]	church [tʃɚ́ːtʃ]

[dʒ]

Initial	Medial	Final
jeep [dʒíːp]	adjective [ǽdʒɪktɪv]	bridge [brídʒ]
joke [dʒóuk]	enjoy [ɪndʒɔ́ɪ]	enlarge [ɪnláɚdʒ]
judgment [dʒʌ́dʒmənt]	religion [rɪlídʒən]	page [péɪdʒ]

音声 39

2.　Phrases

chirp cheerfully—The birds started to chirp cheerfully.

a stage manager—Jack Jones is a fine stage manager.

no major changes—The revision of the tax laws brought no major changes.

3. Contrast

[ʃ]—[tʃ]—[ʤ]

sheep—cheap—jeep

sherry—cherry—Jerry

shin—chin—gin

[ʤ]—[ʒ]

virgin—version

pledger—pleasure

4. Extended practice

A.   Chester Cheetah chews a chunk of cheap cheddar cheese.

(Tongue twister)

B.   How much wood would a woodchuck chuck,

If a woodchuck could chuck wood?

(Tongue twister)

C.   Georgie Porgie, pudding and pie,

Kissed the girls and made them cry;

When the boys came out to play,

Georgie Porgie ran away.

(Nursery rhyme)

5. Conversation

John: Do you know the bridge that's just at the edge of this village?

Jessica: You mean the bridge near the cheese shop?

John: No, Jessica, the other one, right beside the church.

Jessica: You mean the bridge where two jeeps crashed in January?

John: I don't know about that, but you often see people catching fish there.

Jessica: Oh, right! I do know the bridge you mean, John!

Lesson 15

[m]—[n]—[ŋ]

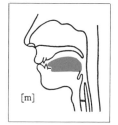 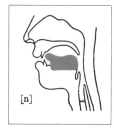 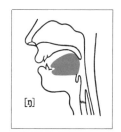

[m] [n] [ŋ] は閉鎖の場所は異なるが([m] は両唇，[n] は歯茎，[ŋ] は軟口蓋)，いずれも口腔に閉鎖がつくられた状態のまま，口蓋垂が下がって呼気が鼻腔に抜ける音である(ゆえに鼻音とよばれる)．/ŋ/ は語中では基本的に [ŋg] となる(例 finger [fíŋgɚ])．但し，形容詞の比較変化を除く派生語尾や活用語尾が綴り字 ng の後ろに続く場合は語中の位置であっても [ŋ] となる(例 singer [síŋɚ])．

1. Words

[m]

Initial	Medial	Final
mail [méɪl]	damp [dǽmp]	autumn [ɔ́:təm]
mall [mɔ́:l]	impossible [ɪmpásəbl]	calm [ká:m]
meet [mí:t]	number [nʌ́mbɚ]	claim [kléɪm]

[n]

Initial	Medial	Final
knife [náɪf]	congratulations [kəngrætʃʊléɪʃənz]	common [kámən]
nail [néɪl]	danger [déɪndʒɚ]	plain [pléɪn]
neat [ní:t]	downtown [dáʊntáʊn]	soon [sú:n]

[ŋ]

Initial	Medial	Final
	angry [ǽŋgri]	king [kíŋ]
	singing [síŋɪŋ]*	long [lɔ́:ŋ]
	stronger [strɔ́:ŋgɚ]*	young [jʌ́ŋ]

*singing [ŋ] と stronger [ŋg] の違いに注意すること．

2. Phrases

homemade jam—Homemade jam tastes better than store-bought jam.

a man of strength—Samson was a man of great strength.

a famous singer—She became a famous singer.

3. Contrast

[m]—[n]—[ŋ]

bam—ban—bang	clam—clan—clang
dim—din—ding	ram—ran—rang
rum—run—rung	some—son—sung

4. Extended practice

To the Dandelion (*excerpt*)

My childhood's earliest thoughts are linked with thee;

The sight of thee calls back the robin's song,

Who, from the dark old tree

Beside the door, sang clearly all day long,

And I, secure in childish piety,

Listened as if I heard an angel sing

With news from Heaven, which he did bring

Fresh every day to my untainted ears

When birds and flowers and I were happy peers.

(by James Russell Lowell)

5. Recognition drills

Listen to the recording and circle the letter of the sentence you hear.

1. [m]—[n]
   a) He had to take a map.
   b) He had to take a nap.

2. [n]—[ŋ]
   a) An old singer came.
   b) An old sinner came.

Lesson 16

[r]—[l]

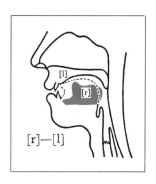

日本語の「ラ」は，舌先を硬口蓋に当ててはじく「瞬間的な音」であるのに対し，英語の [l] や [r] は「継続的な音」である．[l] は舌先をしっかりと上歯茎に触れさせるのに対し，[r] は舌の奥の両脇が奥歯に触れるように発音する．

1. Words

[r]

Initial	Medial	Final*
racket [rǽkɪt]	breeze [bríːz]	
regular [régjʊlɚ]	dry [dráɪ]	
wrap [rǽp]	threat [θrét]	

[l]

Initial	Medial	Final
lap [lǽp]	building [bíldɪŋ]	growl [gráʊl]
little [lítl]	cluster [klʌ́stɚ]	legal [líːg(ə)l]
loan [lóʊn]	split [splít]	rule [rúːl]

2. Phrases

a reading lamp—Where can I get a reading lamp?

very late—It's getting very late.

a relevant reply—He never gives me a relevant reply.

a sprinkle of rain—There was a sprinkle of rain during the night.

---

*本書では [ɚ] を用いることから，語末の [r] はない．

3. Contrast

[r]—[l]

river—liver	grass—glass
right—light	correct—collect
rock—lock	fry—fly
road—load	pray—play
wrong—long	grow—glow

4. Conversation

Mrs. Lawson: Okay, boys and girls, let me collect your papers now.

Larry: Mrs. Lawson, after you collect the papers, are you going to correct them?

Mrs. Lawson: Of course, Larry. I don't just collect them, I always correct them, too, don't I?

Larry: Oh, that's right! You highlight the wrong places in red, and always give us long comments of encouragement!

5. Recognition drills

Listen to the recording and circle the letter of the sentence you hear.

[r]—[l]

1. a) That's quite right.
   b) That's quite light.

2. a) We need to find the rock.
   b) We need to find the lock.

3. a) It's growing.
   b) It's glowing.

4. a) Your answers are all wrong.
   b) Your answers are all long.

5. a) Look at the beautiful grass!
   b) Look at the beautiful glass!

6. a) I saw him praying.
   b) I saw him playing.

7. a) I saw a big crowd yesterday.
   b) I saw a big cloud yesterday.

8. a) Take this road.
   b) Take this load.

Lesson 17

[h]

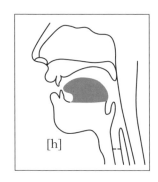

[h] は日本語の「ハ」「ヘ」「ホ」の子音とほぼ同じと考えてよい．日本語の「ヒ」「フ」の子音は [h] ではなく，それぞれ摩擦がより強い [ç] [ɸ] を用いるため，[iː], [ɪ] や [uː], [ʊ] が後続する際の [h] の発音は特に注意を要する．

1. Words

Initial	Medial	Final
harmony [háɚməni]	ahead [əhéd]	
hemisphere [hémɪsfɪɚ]	behave [bɪhéɪv]	
high [háɪ]	perhaps [pɚhǽps]	
whose [húːz]	rehearse [rɪhɚ́ːs]	

2. Phrases

a hard time—They had a hard time of it.

head over heels—Henry fell down the stairs head over heels.

five horses—They own five horses in Hokkaido.

somewhat hastily—Helen had to move somewhat hastily.

3. Contrast

[h]—[f]   [hw]—[w]

hair—fair   head—fed   whale—wail

heat—feet   home—foam   whether—weather

hence—fence   hire—fire   wheel—weal

honey—funny

4. Extended practice

音声
53

Hot cross buns!

Hot cross buns!

One a penny, two a penny,

Hot cross buns!

Hot cross buns!

Hot cross buns!

If you have no daughters,

Give them to your sons.

〈Nursery rhyme〉

5. Recognition drills

Listen to the recording and circle the letter of the sentence you hear.

[h]—[f]

1. a) He hired her.
   b) He fired her.

2. a) You have to hold it.
   b) You have to fold it.

3. a) It was a great hit.
   b) It was a great fit.

4. a) This is a honey bottle.
   b) This is a funny bottle.

5. a) I hear she can't come back.
   b) I fear she can't come back.

6. a) Look up the word *height* in your dictionary.
   b) Look up the word *fight* in your dictionary.

〈コラム〉　　**英語の黙字（Silent Letters）**

音声
54

　英語は音と綴りが一致しない言語として一般的によく知られているが，このズレを生じさせる要因の１つに，発音されない文字，すなわち「黙字」の存在が挙げられる．

Pay careful attention to the silent letters and practice saying the following words:

'b' climb, doubt, lamb, thumb　'g' campaign, design, foreign, gnaw

'k' knee, knife, knock, knuckle　'p' cupboard, pneumonia, psychology, receipt

Lesson 18

[j]—[w]—[hw]

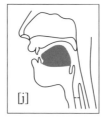
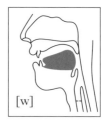

[j] は日本語の「ヤ」,「ユ」,「ヨ」の子音部分に近い．[w] は日本語の「ワ」の子音の
部分よりも唇を丸める．アメリカの一部の地域では，*wh* を含む語を [hw] ではなく，
[w] を用いて発音する場合がある．

1. Words

[j]

Initial	Medial	Final
year [jíɚ]	cure [kjúɚ]	
yesterday [jéstɚdèɪ]	familiar [fəmíljɚ]	
you [júː, jʊ]	interview [íntɚvjùː]	

[w]

Initial	Medial	Final
wax [wǽks]	dwell [dwέl]	
weak [wíːk]	question [kwέstʃən]	
wood [wúd]	switch [swítʃ]	

[hw]

Initial	Medial	Final
whale [hwéɪl]	anywhere [énihwèɚ]	
when [hwέn]	nowhere [nóʊhwèɚ]	
which [hwítʃ]	somewhat [sʌ́mhwàt]	

40

2. Phrases

a few years—I lived in the States for a few years.

a woolen sweater—When winter came, my mother sent me a woolen sweater.

white yarn—It was knit with a lot of white yarn imported from England.

the 5 *w*'s (*who, what, where, when, why*)—The 5 *w*'s of good news reporting are
who, what, where, when, and *why*.

3. Contrast

[j]—[ø]*	[w]—[ø]*	[hw]—[w]
ycast—cast	woos—ooze	which—witch
yolk—oak	woe—oh	whether—weather
yearn—earn	weasel—easel	whet—wet
cue—coo	swoop—soup	
feud—food	square—scare	

4. Extended practice

A.   Compensation

  Why should I keep holiday

  When other men have none?

  Why but because, when these are gay,

  I sit and mourn alone?

  And why, when mirth unseals all tongues,

  Should mine alone be dumb?

  Ah! late I spoke to silent throngs,

  And now their hour is come.

     (by Ralph Waldo Emerson)

〈コラム〉 **Ralph Waldo Emerson** ラルフ・ワルド・エマーソン
(1803 年 5 月 25 日—1882 年 4 月 27 日)

アメリカ合衆国の思想家, 哲学者, 作家, 詩人, エッセイスト. 代表作に, 『自然論』『代表偉人論』『自己信頼』などがある.

---

*[ø] は [j] や [w] がないことを表す([ø] という発音記号はない).

B.   Why do you cry, Willie?

      Why do you cry?

      Why, Willie? Why, Willie?

      Why, Willie? Why?

              （Tongue twister）

      You know New York,

      You need New York,

      You know you need unique New York.

              （Tongue twister）

〈コラム〉　　　　　　　**Hooked schwa [ɚ]**

　フック付きのシュワー（hooked schwa）は，アメリカの音声学者 John S. Kenyon が考案した記号である．シュワーは曖昧母音とも呼ばれ，発音記号は小文字の e を逆さにした [ə] である．シュワーの右肩にあるフックは /r/ を表す記号であることから，フック付きのシュワーは，アメリカ英語の特徴である r 音性を含む曖昧母音の音価を表している（例：bird, girl, nurse, turn の下線部）．加えて，アメリカ英語には，以下に挙げたような r の音色を持つ 5 種の「r の二重母音」と呼ばれるものもある：

/ɪɚ/　b**eer**, cash**ier**, f**ear**, souven**ir**, sph**ere**

/ɛɚ/　b**ear**, c**are**, h**air**, sc**arce**, th**eir**, th**ere**

/ɑɚ/　**ar**m, baz**aar**, h**eart**, s**er**geant

/ɔɚ/　c**our**se, fl**oor**, g**or**geous, r**oar**, w**ar**m

/ɚ/　c**ure**, g**our**met, p**oor**

　一部の英和辞典や英語教科書では，使用する発音記号の数を増やさない工夫として，[ɚ] の代わりにシュワーとイタリック体の r の連字を用いて [əːr] や [ər] と表記することがある．しかし，2 つの記号を用いることで，本来は単母音であるはずの [ɚ(ː)] があたかも 2 つの音の連続であるかの誤解を学習者に与えると批判する研究者もいる．このような誤解を与えないために，上付き r を用いる場合もある（[əʳ]）．

英語の母音

Lesson 19

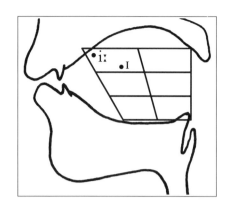

[iː] は日本語の「イ」に近いが，唇をさらに左右に開き，唇を緊張させながら発音する．[ɪ] は [iː] とは音質的にまったく異なる音で，緊張度も弱く，舌の位置も後ろ寄りで低い．

1.   Words

[iː]

Initial	Medial	Final
east [íːst]	field [fíːld]	absentee [æ̀bs(ə)ntíː]
Easter [íːstɚ]	leave [líːv]	ski [skíː]
evening [íːvnɪŋ]	people [píːpl]	tree [tríː]

[ɪ]

Initial	Medial	Final
image [ímɪʤ]	business [bíznəs]	
innocent [ínəs(ə)nt]	river [rívɚ]	
instant [ínstənt]	women [wímən]	

2.   Phrases

three women—Three women were chatting in the hall.

a speech clinic—He went to a speech clinic.

a big machine—He moves like a big machine.

keen competition—There was keen competition for the job.

3.　Contrast

[iː]—[ɪ]

eat—it	feet—fit
beater—bitter	keen—kin
leave—live	heal—hill
sleep—slip	deed—did
sheep—ship	feel—fill

4.　Extended practice

> Hey! diddle, diddle,
>
> The cat and the fiddle,
>
> The cow jumped over the moon;
>
> The little dog laughed to see such sport,
>
> And the dish ran away with the spoon.
>
> (Mother Goose)

5.　Recognition drills

Write down the phonetic spelling of the words you hear.

[iː]—[ɪ]

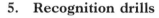

1.　Did you { a. [f__l] / b. [f__l] / c. [f__l] } it?

2.　He bought a { a. [ʃ__p]. / b. [ʃ__p]. / c. [ʃ__p]. }

3.　When did you { a. [l__v] / b. [l__v] / c. [l__v] } there?

4.　Don't { a. [sl__p]. / b. [sl__p]. / c. [sl__p]. }

5.　The boy { a. [b__t] / b. [b__t] / c. [b__t] } it.

6.　They { a. [h__d] / b. [h__d] / c. [h__d] } it carefully.

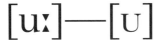

Lesson 20

$$[\mathrm{u\!:}]-[\mathrm{\upsilon}]$$

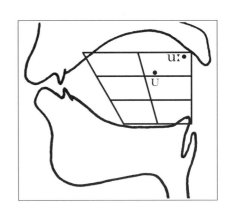

[uː] は口笛を吹く要領で, 唇を丸くして前につき出して発音する. 日本語の「ウ」は唇を丸くしないで発音するので [uː] とはかなり異なる. [ʊ] は高母音としてはやや低い位置で発音される音で, 「ウッ」というつもりで発音する.

1.　Words

[uː]

Initial	Medial	Final
oolong [úːlɔːŋ]	lose [lúːz]	canoe [kənúː]
oops [úːps]	recruit [rɪkrúːt]	crew [krúː]
ooze [úːz]	tool [túːl]	through [θrúː]

[ʊ]

Initial	Medial	Final
	bosom [búzəm]	
	foot [fút]	
	put [pút]	

2.　Phrases

music school—Both girls go to music school.

sugar cookies—Would you like some more sugar cookies?

push and pull—We pushed and pulled, but we could not open the door.

3. Contrast

[ʊ]—[uː]

would—wooed   look—Luke

full—fool   pull—pool

hood—who'd

4. Extended practice

Duke is a foolish mule.

Even his friends admit he's a fool.

One day he tried to stand on a stool,

To look down at a duck in the pool.

But he couldn't because he's a mule—

Duke indeed is a great big fool!

5. Conversation

Luke: Hi Ruth! Where are you going?

Ruth: Hi Luke! I'm going to the swimming pool.

Luke: Are you going to the one near the bookstore?

Ruth: No, it's by the football stadium, just around the corner from the new fruit shop.

Luke: Fruit shop? I didn't know there was a fruit shop nearby.

Ruth: It's brand new, and the fruit's delicious! I'll never buy fruit from the supermarket again!

6. Recognition drills

Write down the phonetic spelling of the words you hear.

[ʊ]—[uː]

1. Are you [f__l]?

2. Have you been [f__lɪŋ] around all day long?

3. I have to $\begin{cases} \text{a.}\,[\text{p\_\_l}] \\ \text{b.}\,[\text{p\_\_l}] \\ \text{c.}\,[\text{p\_\_l}] \end{cases}$ them.   4. Look at the $\begin{cases} \text{a.}\,[\text{s\_\_t}]. \\ \text{b.}\,[\text{s\_\_t}]. \\ \text{c.}\,[\text{s\_\_t}]. \end{cases}$

Lesson 21

$$[\varepsilon]—[æ]—[eɪ]$$

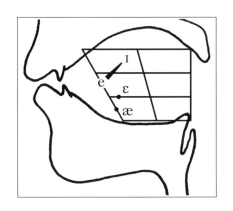

[ɛ] は日本語の「エ」よりも口をやや広めにあけて発音する. 多くの英和辞典などでは [e] の記号で代用することも多い. [æ] は日本語の「ア」の口構えのまま, 唇を横に引き, 緊張をさせた状態で発音する. [eɪ] の第 1 要素 [e] は主音として強く, 長く, 大きめの音量で発音し, 第 2 要素 [ɪ] は副音として, より弱く, 短く, 小さめの音量で発音する.

1.　Words

[ɛ]

Initial	Medial	Final
any [éni]	breath [brɛ́θ]	
edge [ɛ́ʤ]	guest [gɛ́st]	
egg [ɛ́g]	said [sɛ́d]	

[æ]

Initial	Medial	Final
answer [ǽnsɚ]	banana [bənǽnə]	
anxious [ǽŋ(k)ʃəs]	imagine [ɪmǽʤɪn]	
apple [ǽpl]	master [mǽstɚ]	

[eɪ]

Initial	Medial	Final
aid [éɪd]	base [béɪs]	pray [préɪ]
ancient [éɪnʃənt]	lady [léɪdi]	they [ðéɪ]
April [éɪprəl]	saint [séɪnt]	weigh [wéɪ]

48

2. Phrases

the last question—Who can answer the last question?

an assembly plant—We have plans for a new assembly plant.

the main guests—The main guests are all well-known scholars.

native language—My native language is Japanese.

3. Contrast

[ɛ]—[æ]	[ɛ]—[eɪ]	[ɛ]—[æ]—[eɪ]
beg—bag	edge—age	lest—last—laced
hem—ham	fed—fade	met mat—mate
pet—pat	let—late	led—lad—laid
shell—shall	wet—weight	wreck—rack—rake
lend—land	get—gate	pest—past—paste

4. Extended practice

A.   Better late than never.

B.   He who laughs last laughs best.

C.   Haste makes waste.

5. Recognition drills

Write down the phonetic spelling of the words you hear.

A.   [ɛ]—[æ]—[eɪ]

1.   I collect [ʃ__lz].

2.   We'll never see the [m__n].

3.   Did you find a [r__k]?

B.   [ɛ]—[æ]

1.   She's got a { a. [p__n]. b. [p__n]. c. [p__n]. }   2.   He's going to { a. [l__nd] b. [l__nd] c. [l__nd] } it.

3.   Everybody { a. [p__ts] b. [p__ts] c. [p__ts] } the dog.   4.   Look at the { a. [h__m]. b. [h__m]. c. [h__m]. }

Lesson 22

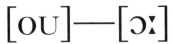 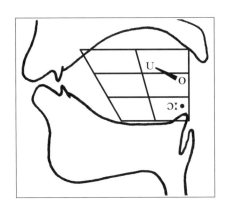

[ou] は口をせばめて発音する [o] から [u] の方へ移る．この [o] は日本語の「オ」よりも位置が高い．[ɔ:] は日本語の「オ」よりもだいぶ低く，緊張を伴って発音される．日本語は，[ou] と [ɔ:] の違いに寛大で，「黄金（おうごん）」を「おおごん」と発音しても別に問題はないが，英語の場合は，意味の違いが生じることもあるので，注意が必要となる．

1. Words

[ou]

Initial	Medial	Final
only [óunli]	cold [kóuld]	sew [sóu]
opening [óup(ə)nɪŋ]	hope [hóup]	though [ðóu]
own [óun]	shoulder [ʃóuldɚ]	window [wíndou]

[ɔ:]

Initial	Medial	Final
all [ɔ́:l]	broad [brɔ́:d]	jaw [ʤɔ́:]
author [ɔ́:θɚ]	fault [fɔ́:lt]	law [lɔ́:]
ought [ɔ́:t]	thought [θɔ́:t]	saw [sɔ́:]

2. Phrases

go home—Let's go home and have supper.

the author's autograph—I got the author's autograph.

the same old coat—He wore the same old coat he had always worn.

3. Contrast

[oʊ]—[ɔː]

音声
69

bowl—ball	boat—bought	row—raw
coat—caught	whole—haul	pose—pause
loan—lawn	choke—chalk	woke—walk
coast—cost		

4. Extended practice

A.

音声
70

Moses supposes his toes-es are roses;

But Moses supposes erroneously;

For nobody's toes-es are posies of roses

As Moses supposes his toes-es to be.

B.

音声
71

My Lost Youth (*excerpt*)

Often I think of the beautiful town

That is seated by the sea;

Often in thought go up and down

The pleasant streets of that dear old town,

And my youth comes back to me.

And a verse of a Lapland song

Is haunting my memory still:

"A boy's will is the wind's will,

And the thoughts of youth are long, long thoughts."

(by Henry Wadsworth Longfellow)

〈コラム〉　　　**二重母音と連母音の違いとは？**

二重母音については研究者間でもさまざまな解釈があり，定義が定まっていないのが実情である．従って，二重母音と連母音の違いを説明するのは意外と難しい．ここでは比較的わかりやすい二重母音の定義を1つ紹介しておこう．二重母音とは「開口度の大きな母音から小さな母音へと転移する」ものをいう（窪薗 1999:149）．従って，アメリカ英語では，上向き二重母音（ei, ai, ɔi, au, ou）ならびに「rの二重母音」*を指すことになろう．これ以外の母音連鎖は連母音とみなされる．

*「rの二重母音」については，Lesson 18のコラム（Hooked schwa）を参照されたい．

Lesson 23

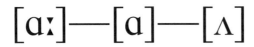

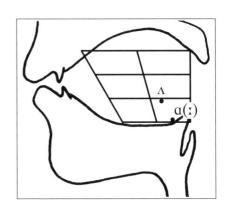

[ɑː] と [ɑ] は英語の音の中でもっとも大きく口を開いて発音する音である．どちらも日本語の「ア」よりも後ろ寄りのやや奥まったところで発音する．イギリス英語では [ɑː] と [ɑ] を区別することが多いが，アメリカ英語の場合，方言によっては両者を区別しないこともある．[ʌ] は口の奥で短く「アッ」というつもりで発音する．

1. Words

[ɑː]

Initial	Medial	Final
ah [áː]	father [fáːðɚ]	grandma [grǽn(d)màː]
almond [áːmənd]	palm [páːm, páːlm]	pa [páː]
alms [áːmz]	psalm [sáːm]	spa [spáː]

[ɑ]

Initial	Medial	Final
honest [ánɪst]	holiday [hálədèɪ]	
honor [ánɚ]	swan [swán]	
olive [álɪv]	what [hwát]	

[ʌ]

Initial	Medial	Final
oven [ʌ́v(ə)n]	bus [bʌ́s]	
ugly [ʌ́gli]	luck [lʌ́k]	
up [ʌ́p]	tunnel [tʌ́n(ə)l]	

2. Phrases

hot chocolate—Do you like hot chocolate?

holiday shopping—I did most of my holiday shopping in November.

another brother—He had another brother named Nathaniel who lived in the
  southern part of Germany.

3. Contrast

[ɑ]—[æ]

hot—hat	mop—map
block—black	gong—gang
fond—fanned	pot—pat

[ʌ]—[ɑ]

color—collar	shut—shot
hut—hot	stuck—stock
luck—lock	

4. Extended practice

Don't dock double-decked duck boats in the double dry docks without paying
  duty.   (Tongue twister)

5. Recognition drills

A.   Write down the phonetic spelling of the words you hear.

[ɑː]—[ɑ]—[ʌ]

1.   My father went to the health [sp__].

2.   He has a [p__t].

3.   Can we take a [b__s]?

B.   Listen to the recording and circle the letter of the sentence you hear.

1. a) I like poppies.   2. a) This collar is beautiful.

   b) I like puppies.   b) This color is beautiful.

Lesson 24

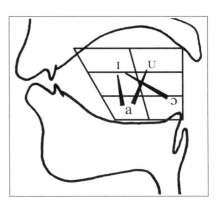

[aɪ] [aʊ] [ɔɪ] などの二重母音は，2 つの単母音の記号を並べて表すが，2 つの音は対等な関係にあるのではなく，第 1 要素の母音（主音）は強く，長く，大きな音量で発音され，第 2 要素（副音）は弱く，短く，小さな音量で発音される．すなわち，第 2 要素の母音は目標点にすぎず，そこまで実際に到達する必要はなく，あくまでも第 1 要素の主音に添えられているものとして考えるとよい．

1. Words

[aɪ]

Initial	Medial	Final
aisle [áɪl]	height [háɪt]	buy [báɪ]
eye [áɪ]	indictment [ɪndáɪtmənt]	sigh [sáɪ]
ice [áɪs]	psychology [saɪkúlədʒi]	supply [səplái]

[aʊ]

Initial	Medial	Final
hour [áʊɚ]	however [hàʊévɚ]	allow [əláʊ]
out [áʊt]	sound [sáʊnd]	anyhow [énihàʊ]
owl [áʊl]	thousand [θáʊz(ə)nd]	bough [báʊ]

[ɔɪ]

Initial	Medial	Final
oil [ɔ́ɪl]	noise [nɔ́ɪz]	boy [bɔ́ɪ]
ointment [ɔ́ɪntmənt]	point [pɔ́ɪnt]	destroy [dɪstrɔ́ɪ]
oyster [ɔ́ɪstɚ]	royal [rɔ́ɪəl]	employ [ɪmplɔ́ɪ]

2. Phrases

oil supply—Our oil supply is running out.

the royal crown—The royal crown was covered with thousands of diamonds.

the high mountain—He guided all the tourists up the high mountain.

a loud voice—He was shouting in a loud voice.

3. Contrast

[aɪ]—[aʊ]—[ɔɪ]

isle—owl—oil

file—fowl—foil

buy—bow—boy

sigh—sow (noun)—soy

4. Conversation

Lloyd: Hi there, Mai! I hear you're going to Owl Island this summer.

Mai: Oh Lloyd, I'm really so excited about it! I've never been to an island before.

Lloyd: Pretty exciting place, I hear. But watch out, you might be attacked by an owl!

Mai: I'm sure owls are harmless just as long as you don't annoy them, but anyhow, thanks for the advice!

5. Recognition drills

Write down the phonetic spelling of the words you hear.

[aɪ]—[aʊ]—[ɔɪ]

1. It's [kw__t] possible.

2. I want to [l__] down.

3. Let's go [d__nt__n].

4. There aren't many [h__ziz] around.

5. The [b__z] and girls are [riʤ__sɪŋ] over the good news.

6. *To the* [l__th__s] was written by Virginia Woolf.

7. The guest was [ʃ__tɪŋ] in a [l__d] [v__s].

Lesson 25

$$[\textrm{ɚ}ː]-[\textrm{ɑɚ}]-[\textrm{ɔɚ}]$$

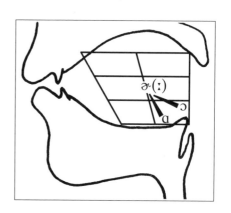

[ɚː] はフック付きシュワー（hooked schwa）とよばれ，曖昧母音 [ə] に小文字の r を右側に付した記号である．アメリカ英語の特徴である r 音性を含む曖昧母音を表すための記号である．多くの英和辞典ではシュワーとイタリック体の *r* の連字が用いられている（[ə*r*]）．[ɑ] や [ɔ] の母音から r に移る際に渡り音として [ə] が挿入されることから [ɑɚ] や [ɔɚ] のように表記するが，それぞれ第 1 要素の母音の箇所を発音する際に，しっかりとあごを開かないと，[ɚ] との区別がつかなくなり，heart [hɑɚt] が hurt [hɚt] に，war [wɔɚ] が were [wɚː] に聞こえてしまうので注意を要する．

1. Words

[ɚː]

Initial	Medial	Final
early [ɚ́ːli]	girl [gɚ́ːl]	fur [fɚ́ː]
earth [ɚ́ːθ]	journey [ʤɚ́ːni]	occur [əkɚ́ː]
irk [ɚ́ːk]	nervous [nɚ́ːvəs]	refer [rɪfɚ́ː]

[ɑɚ]

Initial	Medial	Final
arch [ɑ́ɚʧ]	farmyard [fɑ́ɚmjɑ̀ɚd]	bizarre [bɪzɑ́ɚ]
argument [ɑ́ɚgjʊmənt]	heart [hɑ́ɚt]	guitar [gɪtɑ́ɚ]
article [ɑ́ɚtɪkl]	sergeant [sɑ́ɚʤənt]	seminar [sémənɑ̀ɚ]

[ɔɚ]

Initial

orbit [ɔɚbɪt]

orchestra [ɔɚkɪstrə]

order [ɔɚdɚ]

Medial

horn [hɔɚn]

quarter [kwɔɚtɚ]

wharf [(h)wɔɚf]

Final

explore [ɪksplɔɚ]

pour [pɔɚ]

war [wɔɚ]

2. Phrases

音声
78

an early bird—You're up already? You're a real early bird!

more and more—More and more women are working nowadays.

carve in the marble—The architect carved his name in the marble.

3. Contrast

音声
79

[ɚː]—[ɑɚ]—[ɔɚ]

burn—barn—born   firm—farm—form   purr—par—pour

curt—cart—court   heard—hard—hoard

4. Extended practice

音声
80

　　　　"Don't hurt the heart that never hurt you,

　　　　'cause the heart you hurt may hurt you, too."

　　　　"Hurt the heart that hurt your heart?

　　　　But how can you hurt the heart that hurt your heart,

　　　　if that heart who hurt your heart is the only heart

　　　　that could fix your broken heart?"

　　　　　　　　　　　　　　　　　　(Tongue twister)

5. Recognition drills

Write down the phonetic spelling of the words you hear.

[ɚː]—[ɑɚ]—[ɔɚ]

1. The road [k__vz] around here.

2. I'm looking for my [p__s].

3. No [ʧ__ʤ] is made for delivery.

4. She bought apples, oranges, pears, and so [f__θ].

5. The children learned many poems by [h__t].

6. I [h__d] about the new [st__].

7. He [w__ks] on a [l__ʤ] [f__m].

57

Lesson 26

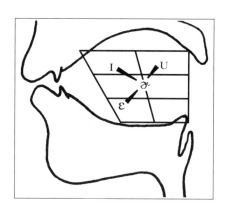

[ɪɚ]–[ɛɚ]–[ʊɚ]

[ɪɚ] の第 1 要素は日本語の「イ」よりもやや口を大きく開けて発音し，舌の筋肉の緊張を解きながら発音する．[ɛɚ] の第 1 要素は日本語の「エ」よりも口を大きく開いて，舌の位置も「エ」よりもかなり低めにし，[ʊɚ] の第 1 要素は日本語の「ウ」よりもやや唇を丸くし，唇の緊張を解いて発音する．いずれも第 1 要素ははっきりと発音し，弱い曖昧母音 [ɚ] に移行する．

1.　Words

[ɪɚ]

Initial	Medial	Final
ear [íɚ]	beard [bíɚd]	atmosphere [ǽtməsfìɚ]
earring [íɚrìŋ]	pierce [píɚs]	engineer [èndʒəníɚ]
earshot [íɚʃàt]	weird [wíɚd]	interfere [ìntɚfíɚ]

[ɛɚ]

Initial	Medial	Final
air [ɛ́ɚ]	scarce [skɛ́ɚs]	despair [dɪspɛ́ɚ]
airplane [ɛ́ɚplèɪn]	therefore [ðɛ́ɚfɔ̀ɚ]	spare [spɛ́ɚ]
airport [ɛ́ɚpɔ̀ɚt]	upstairs [ʌpstɛ́ɚz]	wear [wɛ́ɚ]

[ʊɚ]

Initial	Medial	Final
	bourgeois [búɚʒwɑː]	boor [búɚ]
	gourmet [gúɚmeɪ]	endure [ɪnd(j)úɚ]
	surely [ʃúɚli]	tour [túɚ]

2. Phrases

queer atmosphere—We sensed the queer atmosphere of the office.

pure air—Pure air is disappearing.

in despair—To be sure, the poor man was in deep despair.

3. Contrast

[ɪɚ]—[ɛɚ]

ear—air	shear—share	beer—bear (bare)
dear—dare	here (hear)—hair	fear—fair (fare)
rear—rare	cheer—chair	peer—pear (pare, pair)

[ɪɚ]—[ʊɚ]

mere—moor	peer—poor
sheer—sure	tier—tour

4. Recognition drills

A.   Listen to the recording. If the word you see in your book matches the word you hear, circle its letter.

[ɪɚ]—[ɛɚ]

1. a) cheer	b) cheer	c) chair
2. a) dare	b) dear	c) dare
3. a) rare	b) rare	c) rear
4. a) here	b) hair	c) hair

B.   Write down the phonetic spelling of the words you hear.

[ɪɚ]—[ɛɚ]—[ʊɚ]

1.   The [b__z] [h__].
2.   [h__z] a [f__wɛl] present for you.
3.   He did much for his [p__z]
4.   Have you got a [sp__] pen?
5.   I'm [ʃ__] she'll [ʃ__] the room with me.
6.   Can't you [h__] me from over [ð__]?
7.   The [p__] woman could not [ɪndj__]her life of [f__].
8.   Curious sounds [p__st] the [__].

主要参考資料

〈辞典〉

Jones, Daniel. 1997. *English Pronunciation Dictionary*. 15th ed. (eds.) Peter Roach and James Hartman. Cambridge University Press.

竹林　滋他編. 2012. *Lighthouse English-Japanese Dictionary*　第6版. 研究社.

〈参考文献〉

Baker, Ann. 1981. *Ship or Sheep? An Intermediate Pronunciation Course: New Edition*. Cambridge University Press.

Collins, Beverley and Inger M. Mees. 2008. *Practical Phonetics and Phonology: A Resource Book for Students 2nd ed*. Routledge.

石黒昭博, 高坂京子, 山内伸幸. 1991. 『発信型実践英語音声学』金星堂.

James, Linda and Olga Smith. 2009. *Get Rid of Your Accent*. Business and Technical Communication Services Limited.

Kachru, Braj B. 1985. "Standards, Codification, and Sociolinguistic Realism: the English Language in the Outer Circle" in R. Quirk and H.G. Widdowson (eds.) *English in the World: Teaching and Learning the Language and Literatures*. Cambridge University Press. 11–30.

Kachru, Braj B. 1992. "World Englishes: Agony and Ecstasy" *Journal of Aesthetic Education* Vol. 30, No.2 *Special Issue: Distinguished Humanities Lecture II*. 135–155.

川越いつえ. 2007. 『英語の音声を科学する』大修館書店.

Koizumi, Setsuko and Mikihiko Sugimori. 1988. *English Pronunciation for Communication*. Nan'un-Do.

窪薗晴夫. 1996. 『日本語の音声』岩波書店.

牧野武彦. 2005. 『日本人のための英語音声学レッスン』大修館書店.

Morrison, Malcolm. 2007. *Clear Speech*. A&C Black.

中尾俊夫. 1989. 『英語の歴史』講談社現代新書.

中尾俊夫（児馬修・寺島迪子編）. 2003. 『変化する英語』ひつじ書房.

中尾俊夫, 寺島迪子. 1988. 『図説英語史入門』大修館書店.

中郷安浩, 中郷　慶. 2000. 『こうすれば英語が聞ける』英宝社.

Smith, Larry. 1983. *Readings in English as an International Language*. Pergamon Press.

竹林　滋. 1996. 『英語音声学』研究社.

竹林　滋　斎藤弘子. 1998.『改訂新版　英語音声学入門』大修館書店.

竹林　滋，渡邊末耶子，清水あつ子，斎藤弘子. 1991.『初級英語音声学』大修館書店.

Vaughan-Rees, Michael. 2008. *Test Your Pronunciation*. Penguin English Guides.

KENKYUSHA
〈検印省略〉

アメリカ英語の発音 教本 〈四訂版〉
American English Pronunciation: A Drill Book

2021 年 11 月 30 日　初版発行　　2023 年 11 月 2 日　4 刷発行

編著者　津田塾大学英語英文学科
　　　　© The Department of English, Tsuda University, 2021

発行者　吉田尚志

発行所　株式会社 研究社

〒102-8152 東京都千代田区富士見 2-11-3

電話　営業 （03）3288-7777 ㈹　編集 （03）3288-7711 ㈹

振替　00150-9-26710

研究社ホームページ　https://www.kenkyusha.co.jp/

印刷所　図書印刷株式会社

装丁・図版(声帯)　明昌堂

イラスト　井上秀一(株式会社 イオック)

ISBN 978-4-327-40176-4 C3082

Printed in Japan

音声吹き込み　　Mary Althaus, Greg Dale, Helen Morrison,
　　　　　　　　Trish Takeda, David Csiszar